Learning and Being

THOUGHTS ON OVERCOMING
PROBLEMS AND LIVING FULLY

By Pilar O. Tan, M.D.

Foreword by
Lawrence J. Nardozzi, M. Div., M.D.

Learning and Being

THOUGHTS ON OVERCOMING PROBLEMS AND LIVING FULLY

By Pilar O. Tan, M.D.

Printed by createspace.com

Learning and Being provides a guide for personal enrichment and success. Dr. Tan has collected a series of meditative lessons that will help you to unlock a rich and fulfilling life. Through its graceful, poetic style, each chapter offers coaching and strategies for strengthening relationships in your life, managing problems, and gaining the keys to individual growth and understanding.

For my children
Edward Dylan and Melin

This text is a series of reflections, which include poetry, and prose that express my knowledge as a physician about stress. It is not intended to diagnose, treat, or cure any condition. The reader is advised to seek assistance from a qualified health-care professional as necessary.

Books may be available at special quantity discounts for bulk purchases for sales promotions, premiums, fundraising, and educational use.

Books may be ordered through booksellers or by contacting:
Pilar O. Tan, M.D.
860 Park Avenue
Elizabeth, NJ 07208
908-403-6680
Visit us online at: www.pilartanmd.com

Printed by Createspace.com

ISBN: 978-0-9909599-3-9(paperback)

Library of Congress Control Number: 2002116303

Acknowledgments

With love and gratitude

To my literary agent – Rajander Philip, for his friendship, invaluable guidance and faith in my work; and his efforts.

To my family-especially my children, and my brother, Jose Mariano Tan, for their love, help and support.

To my friends-especially Ting Ting Cheng, Marlene Golab, Arthur Lim, Virginia Long and Larry Nardozzi for their help and special ways of influencing my thoughts in writing this book.

To Marlene Golab, Claire Manfredi and Jane Weiner-for their generosity and friendship.

To my patients and their families-who have inspired me to write this book.

To my office staff-Josephine Palang, Ann Marie O'Keefe, KarynO'Keefe and Melissa Pellicer, for their help.

Above all, to almighty God-who made this task possible.

"*He who knows nothing loves nothing. He who can do nothing understands nothing. But he who understands also loves, notices, sees ... The more knowledge is inherent in a thing, the greater the love ...*"

-Paracelsus

Contents

Foreword

I have had the pleasure of knowing Dr. Tan for many years. Hers is a gentle soul and a genteel demeanor. This essay is undoubtedly gleaned from her many experiences – as a devoted mother, compassionate physician, generous friend and a charitable neighbor. It is a reflection of her spiritual life and devotion. This glimpse into her soul is a gift she gladly shares with us, and it is a gift for which I am grateful.

These musings speak quietly of a life of rectitude lived within the sensitivity of a poet. A proud mother, she has two successful children-one a classical pianist and medical student, the other a lawyer. Dr. Tan continues to demonstrate the highest commitment to the practice of medicine and the cure of her patients. She is a caring and supportive friend. My hope is that others may come to appreciate the beauty and power of her words. *Learning and Being* is a gift from one soul to another.

Lawrence J. Nardozzi, M.Div., M.D.
Priest and Psychiatrist

Chapter 1:

Positive Mental Attitude

"... every individual has the power to establish and control his own mental attitude and direct his power of thought to any desired end, including the absolute control of his reaction to all experiences of his life."

-Napoleon Hill

"Attitude are more important than facts."

-Karl Menninger, M.D.

Positive thinking is a form of though which habitually looks for the best results from the worse conditions... And the remarkable fact is that when you seek good, you are very likely to find it.

-Norman Vincent Peale

Chapter 1:
Positive Mental Attitude

I have learned
that as long as we live
we encounter problems.
Isn't life really
about problem-solving
in the ways that suit us best?

I have learned
that we can profit our problems
when we have a positive mental attitude.

Learning and Being

I have learned
that a positive attitude means
maintaining self-love and self-esteem.
No matter how busy we are
we must take the time
to nurture ourselves each day.

I have learned
that a positive attitude means continuous growth
making and remaking ourselves
like painting and repainting
our own landscapes.

Positive Mental Attitude

I have learned
that a positive attitude
means accepting the pain,
disappointment and loss
that are part of the human condition.

I have learned
that a positive attitude
means accepting that life is difficult
in spite of life's joys and rewards.
My mother used to tell me, "Remember that life is Hard."

I have learned
that positive attitude
means counting our blessings
all the time.
Counting our Blessings
enhances our sense of well-being.

Learning and Being

I have learned
that a positive attitude
means concentrating on what we have,
not what we do not have.

I have learned
that a positive attitude
means seeing the advantages
for every disadvantage.
a cousin of my friend who was born deaf
became a brilliant writer by turning adversity to his favor.

Positive Mental Attitude

I have learned
that a positive attitude
means loving even the unlovable
like loving the gloomy days.

I have learned
that a positive attitude
means focusing on what is good,
true and beautiful
in each moment of our lives.
I say this to my patients,
especially those staying at the hospital.

Learning and being

I have learned
that a positive attitude
means compassion.
When our hearts soften
the logical part of our brains sees things more clearly.

I have learned
that a positive attitude
means seeing what is lovable in others.
What we see influences our interaction with others.

I have learned
that a positive attitude
means doing good things for others.
Giving makes us grow.

Positive Mental Attitude

I have learned
that a positive attitude
requires self-discipline,
honestly and responsibility.
Our ability to have a positive attitude increases
as we develop our love for who we are.

I have learned
that a positive attitude
requires self-knowledge, trust
and forgiveness.
We believe in who we are,
learn from and forgive our past mistakes.

I have learned
that positive attitude
requires creative problem-solving,
perseverance and practice
as in gardening, carpentry or pottery.

Learning and Being

I have learned
that a positive attitude
means being our own best friend,
like how our favorite pet
might treat us.

 I have learned
that we are our own best friend
when we unconditionally accept,
encourage and love ourselves.

I have learned
that we are our own best friend
when we keep doing things
that allow us to like ourselves.

Positive Mental Attitude

I have learned
that we are our own best friend
when we live each moment mindfully.
Let us put our hearts and minds
into whatever we are doing.

Learning and Being

I have learned
that we are our own worst enemy
when we are lazy.
We are not living
when we are not exerting effort to grow.

I have learned
that we are own worst enemy
when we are fearful of living fully.
We can ask ourselves, "Why am I afraid?"
"What is the worst thing that can happen?"

Chapter 2:

Happiness

Someday, after mastering the winds, the waves, the tides, and gravity, we will harness for God the energies of love and then, for the second time in the history of the world, man will have discovered fire.

-Pierre Teilhard De Chardin

"A pleasant and happy life does not come from external things; man draws from within himself, as from spring, pleasure and joy."

-Plutarch

Chapter 2:
Happiness

I have learned
that feelings manifest
the quality of our lives
the way that sweetness reveals
the ripeness of fruit.

I have learned
that the quality of our lives
depends on virtues.
(love, fortitude, prudence,
temperance and justice).
Virtues create a good life.

I have learned
that the quality of our lives
depends on our mental attitude.
Positive mental attitude affects our life's journey.

Learning and Being

I have learned
that we must strive to continuously grow
to achieve happiness.
A peach tree needs time to grow
before it bears fruit.

Happiness

I have learned
that inner happiness
means being our real selves.
If we are a rose
we will not achieve happiness
if we are living as a hyacinth.

Learning and Being

I have learned
that when we are happy
all our problems
become easier to solve.

I have learned
that when we are happy,
we can easily forget ourselves
and focus on selfless things.

I have learned
that peace and happiness
show in our eyes.
Our eyes tell the truth.

I have learned
that happiness and love
are twins
enhancing each other
like two sunflowers
that are growing on one stem.

Happiness

I have learned
that true happiness, like true love,
is an achievement;
a product of personal growth.
We can ask ourselves, "Am I happy now?"
"Do I always feel happiness in my soul?"
"Have I still have some maturing to do?"

Learning and Being

I have learned
that the happiest people
are those who achieve
peace and joy in their hearts.
Have you known people
who exude peace and beauty?

I have learned
that happiness, like love,
is within us,
not someplace else.

I have learned
that we are responsible
for our own life
and our own happiness.
If we rely on other people
for our happiness,
we will never become happy.

Chapter 3:

Human Nature

"When you experience your wisdom and the power of things as they are, together, as one, then you have access to tremendous vision and power in this world. You find that you are inherently connected to your own being. That is discovering magic."

-ChogyamTrungpa

"... inner nature is good or neutral rather than bad, it is best to bring it out and to encourage it rather than to suppress it. If it is permitted to guide our life, we grow healthy, fruitful and happy."

-Abraham H. Maslow

"To the symmetrical nature religion is indeed a crown of glory; nevertheless, so far as this world is concerned, they can grow and prosper without it. But to the unsymmetrical natures religion is a necessary condition of successful work even in this world."

-Lord Acton

Chapter3:
Human Nature

I have learned
that we are all imperfect
and that no human life is perfect
in its entirety.

I have learned
that if we lack a penetrating vision or understanding
we often miss what is good for us.
Have you thought of things you wished you had known
before?

I have learned
that everything in life changes
like the sky.
We should savor each moment fully
for everything is so temporary.

Learning and Being

I have learned
that if we are conscious of the fragility
of our own lives,
we learn to live truthfully.

I have learned
that what is in our heart
is more important
than how we look.

I have learned
that we can bloom
each day like the day lilies.

I have learned
that we are here only for a short time
so we ought to get rid
of unimportant things fast.
We can ask ourselves, "Are the things I am doing
really the important things in my life?"

Human Nature

I have learned
that we are both good and evil
but we can choose
what we want to be.

I have learned
that if we go by the Golden Rule-
"treat others the way
you want them to treat you"-
we do more good than harm

I have learned
That if we can love God
and our neighbors as ourselves
we do not need other rules.

I have learned
that compassion purifies our soul
like fresh air by the sea.

I have learned
that if we understand
we can forgive.

I have learned
that only when we place ourselves
in another's life
can we have real understanding.

I have learned
that when we forgive ourselves
or someone else
we give ourselves a gift.
Have you been generous
to yourself recently?

Human Nature

I have learned
that each time we fall
we learn and lift ourselves
so we can walk again.

I have learned
that in the midst of struggle
we discover amazing things
about ourselves.
It was after my marriage ended
over twenty years ago
that I realized I can do many things well.

I have learned
that we can free ourselves
from unhealthy habits
and use that energy instead
for constructive love and work.

Learning and Being

I have learned
that when we develop
our emotional maturity
or emotional intelligence
we better our lives.

I have learned
that emotional maturity
means knowing ourselves, living courageously
and finding the will to move past
our frustration and disappointments.

I have learned
that emotional maturity
means the capacity
to regulate our moods
and manage our feelings.
One day, I received a deeply moving letter
right before my office hours began.
Regard for my patients made me
postpone the emotional impact
of this letter until I had taken care of them.
Only after I closed the office door did
the tears start to flow.

I have learned
that emotional maturity
means the ability to empathize
and relate with others.
The more we understand
the better our relationships become.

Human Nature

I have learned
that emotional maturity
means being responsible
and having self-discipline.

I have learned
that emotional maturity
means the ability to hope, to handle reality constructively
and to have faith.

I have learned
that emotional maturity
means the ability to love.

Learning and Being

I have learned
that we need to be creative as well as pragmatic
to live well.

I have learned
that art heals and nurtures
our body and soul.

Chapter 4:

Work

"There is nothing training cannot do. Nothing is above its reach. It can turn bad morals to good, it can destroy bad principles and recreate good ones; it can lift men to angelship."

-Mark Twain

"I do the best I know how, the very best I can, and I mean to keep doing so until the end."

-Abraham Lincoln

Chapter 4:
Work

I have learned
that all our dreams
may not come true.
The seeds we plant
may not grow at all.

I have learned
that throughout life
it is good always to have a dream
and a goal to work toward.

I have learned
that throughout life
it is good always to have a dream
even if some dreams that come true
may not bring us the fulfillment that we want.

I have learned
that throughout life
it is through our work and relationships
that we realize who we are.
What do you think made you who you are today?

Learning and Being

I have learned
that most of the time
it is never too late
to be and to do what we want.
Grandma Moses started to paint in her seventies.

I have learned
that if we want something
we have to work and earn it.
What we want does not come free, right?

Work

I have learned
that successful people manage
their time and relationships well.

I have learned
that successful people use the time
when they usually function at their best
for their most important activities.

I have learned
that successful people find a way
to overcome many obstacles
along the way like the persistence
of the sequoia trees.

I have learned
that when we have done our best
some things will fall in place.
When we have done our best,
doesn't something great often
just happen?

Learning and Being

I have learned
that great things start small
like a flicker of light in the dark.

I have learned
that great things
are not done alone.
Look at the great things around you:
How many people accomplished the work?

Work

I have learned
that to lead
we must be strong, a visionary,
a great student and a great teacher.
Good leaders inspire
and bring out the best in people.

Learning and Being

I have learned
that if we do not use our intelligence
we are living inside a home with unlit rooms.

I have learned
that most things that are worth doing
require motivation, perseverance,
patience and practice.
We can achieve
what we really want in life
if we are inspired,
patient and persistent until
we accomplish our goals.

I have learned
that we must find the work
we are meant to do-
something that combines our intelligence and passion.
Our intelligence takes many forms-
perceptual, bodily-kinesthetic, logical-mathematical,
linguistics, musical and visual-spatial.
We often have more than one kind of intelligence.
What is so great is that we often develop a passion
for doing what we are naturally gifted for.

Work

I have learned
that our hearts know
when we are traveling
the right path
because things will just feel right.

I have learned
that a special feeling arises
from accomplishing a difficult task.

I have learned
that it takes positive energy
to continue in the direction
of our soul's desire.
It takes love, does it not?

Learning and Being

I have learned
that when we are inspired
or love what we do
work becomes play.
Have you ever done some work
that you can do for hours without getting worn out
while others can only work for a short time?

I have learned
that it takes creativity to simplify work
and emotional maturity
to live simply.

I have learned
that success means attaining goodness,
wisdom, peace and inner happiness
more so than material things, power or fame
Why are some people who are rich, powerful and famous
so desperately unhappy? What is really important in life?

Work

I have learned
that our children need unconditional love,
support, security, freedom and responsibility.
Raising children is one of the hardest things to do well.

I have learned
that we must take the time
to know each of our children
in order to nurture and respect their unique selves.

I have learned
that we must give our children
our love but we must not expect them
to live their lives the way
we would like them to.

I have learned
that we mostly influence our children
by who and what we are-
not by what we tell them.
Someone telling us that it is snowing
can never compare to the actual experience of the snowfall.

Work

I have learned
that if our children choose to be like us
we have made ourselves well.

I have learned
that when we are raising our children
we have to look at things in the long-term.
What we do for our children in each moment
often has long-term consequences.

Learning and Being

I have learned
that we must give our children the opportunity
to learn, to tolerate frustration,
and develop love and discipline.
Watching our children make mistakes
and experience pain is difficult,
yet we ought not to deprive them
of these vital opportunities to develop
their maturity.

I have learned
that if we want to be like our children
we have done a great job.

I have learned
that we can be many things
to our children:
We can be a parent, a friend,
a colleague or a playmate

Work

I have learned
that to be balanced
and to have a balanced life –
love, work, rest and play must be present
in our lives.
These are teachings passed down to us
by those who are wise.

I have learned
that happiness with our work
more often than not
goes hand in hand with a happy personal life.

Learning and Being

I have learned
that to be true to ourselves
is the only way to live.
It is the only life we have-
let us not waste it.

I have learned
that the only thing that truly belongs
to us is our own life.
We do not own anybody else,
not even our children.

Chapter 5:

Maturity

"*Maturity... it is a continual state of becoming, and it is shown as one deals wisely with the phenomena of one's life.*

... a person of modest IQ but real maturity can get more life - success than can a genius lacking in maturity."

-Louis Binstock

Chapter 5:
Maturity

I have learned
that it takes courage
to be who we truly are.
When we are true to ourselves
others can think
we are living as a fool.

I have learned
that it takes fortitude
to endure, change and manage
work and pain.

I have learned
that fortitude is developed
by adapting maturely to life.

Learning and Being

I have learned
that mature adaptation to life
means healthy or constructive thinking.
How we think shapes our world.

I have learned
that maturity means
our ability to love
ourselves and others constructively.
constructive love is food for our body and soul.

I have learned
that maturity stems from
our ability to navigate within ourselves
and our world realistically
and to the best of our ability.

Maturity

I have learned
that self-love, self-esteem,
mature adaptation and spirituality
are pillars of maturity.

I have learned
that if we did not develop our spirituality
early in life
we hopefully develop it later on
as we grow and mature.

Learning and Being

I have learned
that our adaptation
to the difficult daily changes in our lives
can be constructive (mature)
or destructive (immature)
to ourselves and/or to others.

I have learned
that immature adaptation to life
causes problems
and covers problems with more problems,
like adding clouds to the sky.
Children who have problems at home
may take drugs, drop out of school or act out in some other
ways.

I have learned
that mature adaptation
is the key to creating a remarkable life.
We turn a disadvantage into an advantage,
create beauty out of pain, etc.,
when we adapt to life maturely.

Maturity

I have learned
that mature adaptation means
having a great sense of humor.

I have learned
that mature adaptation means
suppression, sublimation,
altruism, anticipation and asceticism.

I have learned
that humor makes painful
or embarrassing experiences easier to bear.
When I remember some
of the embarrassing experiences that I have had
I just laugh at myself.

Maturity

I have learned
that suppression means that at any time
we can choose what to think, what we desire,
what to feel and what to do;
we are the master of ourselves.
After discussing a disturbing incident,
my daughter, preparing for a difficult medical school
examination, told me,
"I am not going to think about it now.
I will think about it after my exam."

Learning and Being

I have learned
that sublimation means we can create
something magnificent out of misfortune
like Beethoven writing the Ninth Symphony
while virtually deaf.
I would probably not have learned
to draw vivid flowers
if I had not had painful things happen in my life.

Maturity

I have learned
that altruism means doing things
that are good for others.
Many charitable organizations are formed
by people who have experienced tragedies
in their lives.

Learning and Being

I have learned
that anticipation means we can foresee
the consequences of our behavior.
Anticipation stops ourselves from destructive acts.
Have you ever said, "I am glad I thought it through it first?"

Maturity

I have learned
that asceticism means denying oneself
pleasure for the sake of a greater cause.
Growing up in the Philippines surrounded by poverty
I witnessed people who were starving
yet happily gave food to their children and relatives.

I have learned
that it takes strength and self-discipline
to get out of a wrong situation
or stop doing destructive things.

I have learned
that suppression, altruism,
anticipation and asceticism
are the ingredients of self-discipline.

Maturity

I have learned
that self-discipline becomes easier to do
if we reward ourselves immediately
after doing difficult things.

I have learned
that love for ourselves and for others
is the motive of self-discipline.

Learning and Being

I have learned
that we are a spiritual being
having a physical body.
Most but not everyone will agree with me on this.

I have learned
that our spirit
is the essence of our being
like the extract of a flower.

I have learned
that spirituality means
believing and being in touch with God
or a higher power.
What would life be without God?

Maturity

I have learned
that spirituality means
fulfilling our need for love and completeness
through the divinity within us.
We should share our love with others
but we should not depend on them
to make us feel whole.

Learning and Being

I have learned
that spirituality means
reverence for life.

I have learned
that spirituality means
living with compassion
and forgiveness.
Have you ever done this
when someone has hurt you?

I have learned
that spirituality means
living with faith, hope and charity.
Religion is part of spirituality
but being religious is not necessarily being spiritual.

Maturity

I have learned
that spirituality means
valuing art, music and nature.

I have learned
that spirituality means
a feeling of community.
We are interdependent
and should help each other.

I have learned
that spirituality means
that we co-create our life with God
as we know God.
Not everything that happens
to us is under our control.

Learning and Being

I have learned
that maturity
is the stepping stone
to self-realization.

I have learned
that maturity
allows us to become
the best that we can be
 and to achieve fulfillment in love and work.

Chapter 6:

Friendship

"What is a friend? A single soul dwelling in two bodies."
-Aristotle

"Friendship redoubleth joys, and cutteth griefs in halves."
-Francis Bacon

Chapter 6:
Friendship

I have learned
that one of the most valuable things
in life is having real friends (philia).

I have learned
that real friends
are like drinking spring water
after a long hike.

I have learned
that we may give to many people
but we have only a few true friends.
How many people can we depend on
during an emergency?

Learning and Being

I have learned
that if we like a certain person
that person probably likes us as well.

I have learned
that if we expect something from others,
even from those who love us,
we make our lives miserable.

I have learned
that when we hold other people's hands
we can prevent them from falling.
Friends can do many things
to help each other.

I have learned
that we can support people
and share our opinion with them
but we must let them solve
their own problems.
We need to respect others for their uniqueness.

Friendship

I have learned
that our close friends may have many similarities
but like sea shells
they may also be very different from each other.

I have learned
that our closest friends
mirror and grow with us.

I have learned
that our closest friends
inspire us to be our best.
Who are the people who have given you
reasons to become your best?

I have learned
that our closest friends
reaffirm our value
for who and what we are.

Learning and Being

I have learned
that knowledge, fondness and trust
come with time,
but once true friendship emerges
it remains with us forever.
If any of us do not have this kind of friendship as yet
let us make the time to keep making friends.
We can ask ourselves,
"Are we spending enough time for ourselves?"

I have learned
that a true friend
glows in our heart
and lights our path.

Chapter 7:

Self-Love

"We shall not cease from exploration and the end of all our exploring will be to arrive where we started and know the place for the first time."

-T.S. Eliot

"There's only one corner of the universe you can be certain of improving; and that's your own self. So you have to begin there, not outside, not on other people. That comes afterwards, when you have worked on your own corner."

-Aldous Huxley

"The nature of this flower is to bloom."

-Alice Walker

Chapter 7:
Self-Love

I have learned
that love begins
with loving ourselves.

I have learned that self-love
means knowing who we truly are,
knowing our unique self.

I have learned
that self-love means being kind to oneself,
making time to nurture our body and spirit.
We need to spend enough time for ourselves each day.

I have learned
that self-love means being patient with oneself
like tending to a garden each day
actively nurturing the flowers to bloom.

Learning and Being

I have learned
that self-love means being compassionate
to ourselves in caring for our own needs
(safety, belonging, love, esteem)
especially when we are in pain.
We have to make ourselves a priority
especially when we are going through difficult times.

I have learned
that self-love means being, knowing, accepting,
supporting and understanding
who we really are.

Self-Love

I have learned
that self-love means having faith in oneself,
trusting one's soul.

I have learned
that self-love means physical, spiritual, emotional
and intellectual responsibility
and self-reliance.
Out of all of the above
emotional self-reliance
was my greatest difficulty to achieve.

Learning and Being

I have learned
that self-love means autonomy;
creating one's destiny
and realizing one's soul.

I have learned
that self-love means becoming
what we want to be.
All of us can become
what we want to be
regardless of our circumstances or past.

I have learned
that self-love means acknowledging
and forgiving weaknesses;
changing what we can
and beginning each day anew.
Part of being human
is making mistakes.

Self-Love

I have learned
that self-love means living consciously;
seeking and living with clarity,
to live purposefully and responsibility.

I have learned
that self-love means
living each moment humbly
with awareness and acceptance.

I have learned
that self-love means living each moment fully
and living that moment
with integrity and reverence.

Learning and Being

I have learned
that self-love means affirming our own life,
strengthening our will to live.
We should uphold our will to live.

I have learned
that self-love means self-discipline
or mastering our way to wholeness.
When we have done something destructive
we must find a way to move past it
and continue to grow.

I have learned
that self-love means
positive mental attitude.

Self-Love

I have learned
that self-love grows
when we exert effort
and harness our courage,
like when we are working hard toward our dream.

I have learned
that self-love grows
when we bring out the best
in ourselves and in others.
Loving others is also loving ourselves.

I have learned
that self-love grows
when we are good, intimate,
giving and forgiving.
self-love grows when we have loving relationships.

Learning and Being

I have learned that
when we discover
love in our heart
and feel its happiness,
our world is transformed.

Chapter 8:

Intimacy

"Being intimate does not occur by serendipity, particularly with persons to whom we are close. . . In close relationships, being intimate requires work. We have to learn, or perhaps relearn, what we have to do to allow it to happen and what we have to avoid doing that prevent it from happening."
-Patrick Thomas Malone, M.D.

"Intimacy is the capacity of two people to offer each other's real selves affection and acknowledgement in a close, ongoing interpersonal relationship."
-James F. Masterson, M.D.

Chapter 8:
Intimacy

I have learned
that intimacy is like drawing –
an art that can be nurtured.

I have learned
that intimacy is a good measure
of the depth and quality of our relationships.

I have learned
that intimacy is the mutual exchange
of souls that are the same level,
like the interchanging water
of the ocean and the lagoon.

Learning and Being

I have learned
that intimacy means sharing
who we truly are,
revealing our deepest thoughts and feelings.

I have learned
that intimacy means being kind and honest
at the same time.
We can learn to be truthful and tactful.

Intimacy

I have learned
that intimacy helps us see
our own truths
so we can face and solve our problems.

I have learned
that intimacy helps our relationships
and each other to grow.

I have learned
that intimacy lessens our pain
and enhances our joy.
Doesn't it feel good to have intimate relationships?

Learning and Being

I have learned
that intimacy requires
work and courage,
it means love in action.

I have learned
that intimacy requires
support and challenge.

I have learned
that intimacy requires
sensitivity, sincerity,
trust and respect.

Chapter 9:

Self-Esteem

"If you are not for you
who will be?
If you are only for you
what's the purpose?
If not now, when?"

- Hillel

"I think one must finally take one's life in one's arms."
-Arthur Miller

Chapter 9:
Self-Esteem

I have learned
that self-esteem evolves
alongside self-love
like great music
arises from a great composer.

I have learned
that self-esteem means
having self-respect
and self-confidence

Learning and Being

I have learned
that self-esteem means
the ability to enjoy people and things
without depending on them
to feel worthwhile.

I have learned
that self-esteem means knowing
deep in our hearts
that we are worthy
of love and happiness.

Self-Esteem

I have learned
that self-esteem requires
that we believe in our own worth
regardless of what other people say.

I have learned
that self-esteem requires
the ability to know our own values
and to actively work towards them.
From time to time
we can ask ourselves, "What do I want?"
"Am I walking on the right path?"

Learning and Being

I have learned
that self-love and self-esteem
are interdependent
like color and light.

I have learned
that when we have adequate
self-love and self-esteem,
we are like gardenias in bloom.

Self-Esteem

I have learned
that things that increase self-love
also increase self-esteem.

I have learned
that when we have
strong self-esteem,
we follow our own bliss.

Chapter 10:

Love

"Love is the only satisfactory answer to the problem of human existence."

-Erich Fromm

"To cheat oneself of love is the most terrible deception, it is an eternal loss for which there is no reparation, either in time or in eternity."

-Kierkegaard

"For one human being to love another: that is perhaps the most difficult task of all..., the work for which all other work is but a preparation. It is a high inducement to the individual to ripen... a great exacting claim upon us, something that chooses us out and calls us to vast things."

-Rainer Maria Rilke

Chapter 10:
Love

I have learned
that we blossom
when someone truly loves us.

I have learned
that sometimes it is easier to know
when someone loves us
that if we love him or her.

Learning and Being

I have learned
that the loss of loved ones tear our hearts
but we can mend our torn hearts.

I have learned
that the word love
means many things.
Here are some of the things called "love":
pleasure, admiration, physical attraction,
fondness, friendship, kindness, respect,
intimacy, patience, support, caring, encouragement,
empathy, understanding, nurturing,
effort, courage, goodness, forgiveness,
altruism and asceticism.

Love

I have learned
that our love can be mature or immature,
like trees in a forest.

I have learned
that the amount and maturity of our love
depend on what lies at our core.

I have learned
that mature love (agape) gives unconditionally
for the joy of giving,
immature love comes with motives.
Mature love is life-enhancing like the warm sun;
immature love inhibits our growth like winter rain.

Learning and Being

I have learned
that the love (eros)
means admiration, respect
and physical chemistry.
This is often called "romantic love."

I have learned
that the ways in which someone treats us
is more important than physical attraction.
Physical attraction withers when there is no respect.

I have learned
that when someone's life becomes
as important as our own,
he or she changed our life.

Love

I have learned
that sexual desire
is many times
not a conscious choice.
"I do not know why I love him or her
but I just do."

I have learned
that sexual desire can be aroused
by instinct, infatuation, excitement,
projection, anger, or the desire to control,
destroy or punish.

I have learned
that sexual desire can be aroused
by real physical chemistry,
the feeling of pleasure in being physically close
to someone.
Have you experienced this?

I have learned
that sexual desire can be aroused
by feelings of love.
Sexual desire grows over time
if our love for each other continues to grow.

Love

I have learned
that true love (eros, agape, philia)
takes time to create,
like painting a magnificent portrait.

I have learned
that true love
is a conscious choice and a constant commitment.
True love is loving the whole person
with our eyes open.

I have learned
that true love means
mutual affirmation
of the value of each other's self.

I have learned
that true love
brings peace and joy
in our hearts.
Have you truly loved someone?

Learning and Being

I have learned
that true love grows
when we are continually intimate
and giving of ourselves.

I have learned
that true love grows
when we share, when we give
and when we practice interdependence.

I have learned
that true love grows when we believe in
and are committed to the relationship.
It takes mutual agreement
to make the bond of love permanent.

Love

I have learned
that true love will not grow
when we do not accept
and understand each other.

I have learned
that true love will not grow
when we become controlling, selfish,
narcissistic or unforgiving.

I have learned
that true love will not grow
when we become destructively dependent, demanding,
dishonest or disrespectful.

I have learned
that the happiness, security and well-being
of our true love
become as important to us as our own life.
Our true love is worth giving the best
of what we are and what we have.

Learning and Being

I have learned
that our true love
is our soul mate.

I have learned
that soul mates work together on every level:
physical, spiritual,
intellectual and emotional.

Love

I have learned
that soul mates walk together
in the same direction.

I have learned
that a soul mate is a true friend
we can count on every time.

Learning and Being

I have learned
that when we are married
to our true love
we are incredibly fortunate.
My parents were very lucky.

I have learned
that fortune is good luck
and hard work.

I have learned
that good luck depends on chance
and emotional maturity.

Love

I have learned
that marriage is the most complex relationship.
It needs to blend many parts
of two people's lives.

I have learned
that marriage can be the most life-enhancing experience.
Growing up, I experienced
that my parents' lives
were enriched by their marriage.

I have learned
that marriage requires sensitivity,
generosity, flexibility, compromise,
creativity and trustworthiness.
We have to become the right person
and be married to the right person.

Learning and Being

I have learned
that even when we are married to our true love
we need to continue to nurture our other relationships.
These relationships—
such as family and friends—
strengthen our marriage.
One person cannot fulfill
all of our emotional needs.

I have learned
that even when we are married to our true love
we need to continue to develop interests that maybe
apart from the relationship.

Chapter 11:

Stress

"Stress is the nonspecific response of the body to any demand made upon it... it is immaterial whether the agent or situation we face is pleasant or unpleasant, all that counts is the intensity of the demand for readjustment or adaptation."

- Hans Selye

"The mind is its own place, and in itself can make a Heav'n of Hell, a Hell of Heav'n."

-John Milton

Chapter 11:
Stress

I have learned
that the most powerful
source of stress is our own mind.
Our mind determines whether
what happens to us is stressful or not.

Learning and Being

I have learned
that we prevent many stressful situations
from happening
when we use mature adaptation
in our life.

I have learned
that mature adaptation
allows us to handle stressful situations
in ways that become
advantageous to us.

Stress

Here are some examples of stressful
situations where people use mature
adaptation to deal with their problems:

1. Humor—

Tom's wife was always reminding him about something but
he never believed that he was forgetful. "You'd forget your
head if it weren't attached to your shoulders.," she would say
to him. One day, after visiting his father in the hospital, Tom's
car suddenly stopped. To his embarrassment, he realized
that he had run out of gas. His only option was to call his wife
to come and pick him up. "Dear," he said when she answered
the phone. "I remembered my head but forgot to get gas
today." They both enjoyed a hearty laugh.

2. Suppression—

Caroline generally spoke on the telephone with her good friend several times a week. One day, without warning, her friend failed to return her calls. While she was very worried, there was little she could do. A few days later, at a social affair, she spotted her friend across the room. She was relieved that her friend was all right but she was also angry at the same time. Caroline was able to disguise her hurt feelings until they had a moment in private when they could speak about this stressful situation.

3. Sublimation—

One of Mary's fondest memories was her playing with her dolls and imagining what it would be like to be a mother. Years later, her disappointment was tremendous when she learned that she could not bear children. She felt very unhappy and depressed until one day when she saw a television program on an agency caring for unwanted children in a poor country. She was so moved by this program that she volunteered her time with the agency. Almost immediately, her depression lifted and she began to feel happy.

John was always a shy person. While he wanted a romantic relationship, he never had the ability to initiate a conversation with a woman without becoming embarrassed and feeling awkward. When he enrolled in a creative writing course, he began to write poetry. Sometime after that, while autographing his first published book, he met a woman and they fell in love.

4. Asceticism—

Nora always dreamed of being a doctor. She imagined herself at patients bedsides in a hospital, relieving their sufferings and helping them to become well. She sacrificed spending weekends at the library studying even on a beautiful day, instead of outdoor activities she loved —hiking or going to the beach; to hopefully get into a good medical school, realize her most cherished dream of becoming a doctor and help people.

5. Altruism

Eleanor, who was eighty years old, volunteered in the nursing home instead of staying home feeling sorry for herself, focusing on her arthritic pain. She said, "I love volunteering, I love helping people and it makes me forget my pain."

6. Anticipation

Jennifer came from a poor family. It was no surprise, therefore, that she had to work her way through college. Whenever she had a free moment at the supermarket checkpoint line, she imagined what her life would be like when she will become a successful corporate lawyer. She has been studying hard because she knows that getting excellent grades will lead to a successful career.

Stress

I have learned
that how we respond to a situation will
determine the outcome of things.

I have learned
that what we choose to see
is what we see.
When we choose to see rose petals
instead of thorns,
it's the rose petals that we will see.

I have learned
that the more we challenge ourselves
the more stressful situation we can handle,
like our muscles becoming stronger
with strengthening exercises.

I have learned
that when we are mature
we can rebound
even from a difficult loss.
A mature dogwood will have new shoots
after we cut some branches.

Stress

I have learned
that an absence of a worthwhile endeavor
makes life more stressful.
When we have problems
and we do not find meaningful things to do
our lives become worse.

Learning and Being

I have learned
that even when we mature
we can become immature
under very stressful conditions.

I have learned
that when we are immature
we lack self-discipline
and cannot love ourselves or others constructively.
Examples of destructive behaviors:
gambling, food, sexual and drug addictions,
delinquency, absenteeism, physical abuse, etc.

Stress

I have learned
that when we are immature
we adapt poorly to life.

I have learned
that poor adaptation
causes more stress.

I have learned
that poor adaptation often leads
to anxiety and depression—
signals that something needs
to be addressed.

I have learned
that stress is a mind and body response
of our nervous system
to a real or imagined threat to ourselves.

I have learned
that stress handicaps our ability to think
and solve our own problems.
Have you ever experienced a time
when you were so stressed out
that your mind became blank?

Stress

I have learned
that stress causes an imbalance in the involuntary or
autonomic nervous system
resulting to an abnormal bodily functions.

I have learned
that signs and symptoms caused by stress
are headache, irritability, lack of concentration,
palpitations, anxiety, depression, abdominal pain,
diarrhea, etc.
All the organs innervated
by the autonomic nervous system
can manifest signs and symptoms of stress.

Learning and Being

I have learned
that common diseases caused by stress
are high blood pressure, heart attack, stroke,
asthma, depression, some forms of cancer
and hyperacidity in the stomach.

Stress

I have learned
that we can live a healthy life
through skillful self-training
even though we are going through
some of life's major stressors,
such as the death of loved one's, major illness, etc.
These behaviors
require time and practice.

I have learned
that these behavioral changes
can include proper diet, physical exercise,
meditation and diaphragmatic breathing.

Learning and Being

I have learned
that there is short-term relief form stress
that we can get, such as getting a massage,
listening to soft music, aromatherapy,
visualization, watching a funny movie,
playing with our pets, playing games,
gardening and talking to those with whom we are intimate.

Stress

I have learned
that when we handle stress well
and balance our autonomic nervous system,
we function optimally,
like balloons rising in the sky.

I have learned
that when we handle
stress well,
we are healthier, we are more productive
and we enjoy intimate relationships and life more.

Chapter 12:

Life

"To be what we are, and to become what we are capable of becoming, is the only end of life."

-Robert L. Stevenson

"The path to sainthood goes through adulthood. There are no quick and easy shortcuts. Ego boundaries must be hardened before they can be softened. One must find one's self before one can lose it."

-M. Scott Peck, M.D.

"The ultimate measure of a successful life could be found by looking at an ability to work and to love."

-Sigmund Freud

Chapter 12:
Life

I have learned
that we need to be in touch
with the reality of our own life.

I have learned
that our life's day-to-day journey matters more
than the end of our journey.
Life is the present moment.

Learning and Being

I have learned
that it is harder to live than to die,
especially when we are ill.
Life itself is hard enough
and when we are ill
it is even worse.

I have learned
that when we are in pain
we must grieve our losses
and find reason to go on.
To grieve, we must go through denial,
anger, depression and acceptance.
Also, we must remind ourselves
of the things we live for.

I have learned
that when we are in pain
we must do everything possible
to heal our soul.
Let the inner spirit shine through.

Life

I have learned
that to keep living
we must keep learning.

I have learned
that throughout our lifetime
we must continuously apply
what we have learned.
It is not enough to know;
we have to use the lessons of life.

I have learned
that the more wisdom
we have on life,
the greater our love.
knowledge influences our love of life.

Learning and Being

I have learned
that people who want to die
have not yet lived.
If someone wants to die
let us show him/her how to live.

I have learned
that to live
we need to be, to do, to endure,
to play and to give.
Ultimately,
life is about giving.

Life

I have learned
that whenever something gives us pleasure at the moment
it is wise to ask ourselves,
"Will this activity harm us three months from now?"

I have learned
that we can mentally label
constructive things as pleasurable
and destructive things as not,
like choosing to love doing physical exercise
and choosing to hate eating high cholesterol food.

Learning and Being

I have learned
that we can live each day
to the best and fullest
giving ourselves the best present every day.

I have learned
that when something bothers us
it is good to ask ourselves,
"Is what I am worrying about really worth it?"
"Will this matter three years from now?"

Life

I have learned
that suffering happens
to everybody.

I have learned
that if we carry our burdens from the past
we may not be able to walk.
We can become handicapped
in our ability to think logically.

I have learned
that our best vacation happens
when we do not need a vacation
from ourselves.

I have learned
that suffering can push us to do evil
or become closer to God.

I have learned
that we are meant to grow
toward what is true,
good and beautiful,
like flowers in the sun.

Life

I have learned
that the greatest pain
can opened our closed eyes.
When in pain
we come to realize
some truths that are hidden in our soul.

I have learned
that when our life hurts
our soul comfort us,
like the sun vanishing the night.

Learning and Being

I have learned
that when we pray
miraculous things occur.

I have learned
that miracles are as abundant
as flowers.
some of my patients have gotten better
even when the prognosis
of their illnesses is poor.

I have learned
that many miraculous things come in threes—
like faith, hope and love;
past, present, and future;
the Trinity and a clover leaf.

Life

I have learned
that when we tell the truth
we make people laugh or cry.
Whenever I call a friend
and tell her "I have something to tell you"
immediately she says "What?" with laughter.

I have learned
that to be able to laugh and cry
are gifts from God.

I have learned
that life is easier
if we can laugh about ourselves.
Having a sense of humor is our best ally.

Learning and Being

I have learned
that if we love dogs or other pets
we have special friends
that comfort and warm our body and soul
for all seasons of our lives.

I have learned
that if we love flowers and music
we love two of the world's
most beautiful things.
What are the things
you consider beautiful in life?

I have learned
that the most beautiful sound
comes from a human voice.

Life

I have learned
that we have to live with the rain and night
and yet live a resilient,
happy and peaceful life—
full of gratitude and awe.

I have learned
that regardless of who we are
and what we have been,
each moment of life begins anew.
Whether we are poor, rich, young,
old, an addict, an executive,
we can become mature.

I have learned
that we can handle life's stressors
by developing maturity
and by living a healthy life style.

Learning and Being

I have learned
that regardless of who we are
we can develop and maintain
our self-love and self-esteem;
able to love, work and enjoy life.

Life

I have learned
that we can be a good person
worthy of all good things.

I have learned
that we are responsible
for making this world a better place.
Others before us made
our modern world today,
now it's our turn
to leave a legacy.

Learning and being

I have learned
that we can live each moment uniquely
and touch each other's lives lovingly.

Glossary

Act out: by avoiding painful feelings by doing impulsive,
                    attention getting activities that are usually destructive.

Adaptation: to change oneself so that one's behavior, attitudes, etc.,
                    will correspond to new or changed circumstances.

Altruism: the principle of living and doing things for the good of
                    others.

Agape: derived from the Greek word "agape" which means
                    spontaneous, altruistic love.

Anticipation: to take or consider the consequences of one's behavior
                    ahead of time

Asceticism: the act of denying oneself pleasure for the sake of a
                    greater good.

Autonomic nervous system: the part of our nervous system that function
without our conscious control. It is activated during stress. It innervates
our eyes, blood vessels, circulation, digestion, glands associated with the
nasal cavity and oral cavity, sweat glands, adrenals, kidneys, reproduction,
respiration and urination. The autonomic nervous system causes
inhibition or stimulation depending on the organs supplied. Imbalance of
inhabitation and stimulation causes signs and symptoms of stress. Doing
abdominal breathing balances stimulation (inspiration) and inhibition
(expiration) thereby relieving ourselves of stress. Although breathing is
regulated by the autonomic nervous system and functions without our
conscious control, one can learn to control breathing consciously through
practice such as during meditation.

Learning and Being

Eros:	"God of love" in Greek mythology.
Fortitude:	the strength to have firm courage and patience when enduring misfortune.
Innervate:	to supply parts of the body with nerves.
Justice:	to employ sound reason, fairness or uprightness.
Prudence:	the ability to think through the consequences of one's action for one's own interest.
Sublimation:	the ability to transform aggressive and socially unacceptable biological drives for a greater social good.
Suppression:	the ability to consciously control one's thought, desire and emotion; and express them at an appropriate time.
Temperance:	a state or quality of self-restraint expression or indulgence of pleasure.

Index

Pilar Tan, M.D. hails from the
Philippines. She is a Diplomate of
the American Board of Internal
Medicine. She has been
practicing as an internist for over
thirty years in Elizabeth, New
Jersey. She currently cares for
four thousand patients ranging in
age from ten to ninety-six. Her
poems have been published in
newsletters and anthologies. She
has given speeches on various
topics, including happiness,
maturity, stress, positive mental
attitude, relationships and work
which are covered in this book.

www.ingramcontent.com/pod-product-compliance
Lightning Source LLC
Chambersburg PA
CBHW071441090426
42737CB00011B/1739